Evolution To Black Reflection In The Mirror

Osiris Halisi

ISBN: 1-4392-3520-1
ISBN-13: 9781439235201

Visit www.booksurge.com to order additional copies.

Poems

63. photo
64. evolution
65. photo

Evolution to Black

Intro

This is my journey from the son of revolutionaries On the frontline of the civil rights movement, To a life stuck in a cycle of violence, the effects of A boy watching his mother slowly fade into the grips Of depression, my life on the hills of Altadena the chill Of Indiana air, the poetry of suicide that lye's in the hopeless mind. My struggle to understand what it means To be black how to move in a land that enslaved my ancestors, and denied my people basic rights. The anger passed threw struggle in a changing world can lead You down the wrong paths. my life up to this point has Been fueled by hate and depression trying to find myself in a world were on mistake can consume so much time Especially if you are African American male. I have made a few, so my evolution has been slow. this is my story before realizing love is the key and hate will eventually kill your soul. I found Life in poetry my therapy written letter to my mother in heaven is my evolution. For me evolution is arriving at point were your past is just that and with real love for your self and humanity you can accomplish anything, so my life begins. Yes we can! A child Us!

The organization

When I say I am the son of a revolutionary, I was born to C.R.D Halisi and Lagary Newton members of US organization one of the powerful black activist groups of the 70's and famed rivals of the black panthers. My father Dr. Halisi was Maulana Karenga's right hand man and one of the great political minds to be produced through the organization, and went on to be a famous professor on south African politics and African American studies. A true revolutionary and soldier for the civil rights movement , but to every success story there's another side (me). My poetry comes from the beginning of the struggle, when him and my mother were young revolutionaries at war with society, and desperate for change in the black communities of California. My memories are of dashikis and bold heads and guns in the closet fully loaded, two moms and a lecture on the way about being black !I sit and day dream about those days often.

Osiris Halisi

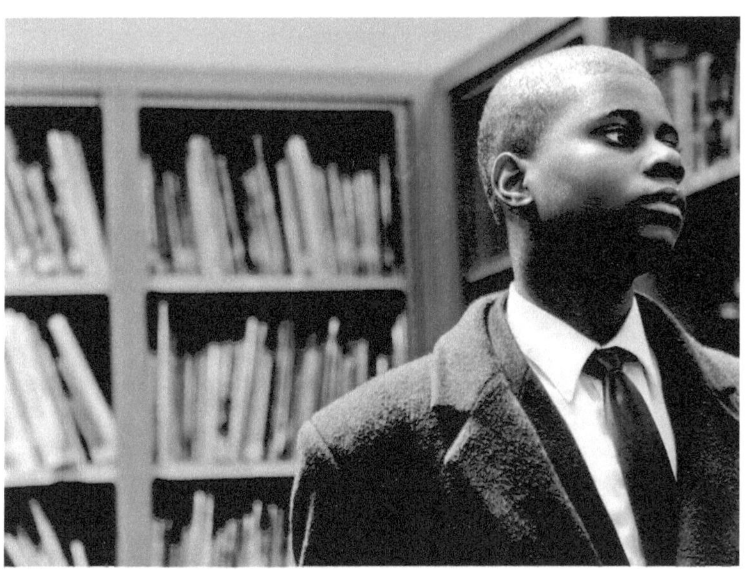

Us (poetry)

Draped in dashikis and bold heads covered
with the colors of the mother land, protected
by hands that hold clips that load guns with
the bullets of change or die that fly pursing the
radical mind that sparks a idea that only knowledge
can bring change.
As a organization begins to speak and teach a
people about it's history, kwanza candles
burn on mantels drip the blood of soldiers
draped in dashikis my father spits fire.
(The son of a revolutionary) Osiris Halisi
Ps.
spawned from the struggle of streets , baptized
in the fight for civil rights , born to scholars
raised by the depressed named after the god
of the dead guided by the wings of angels.

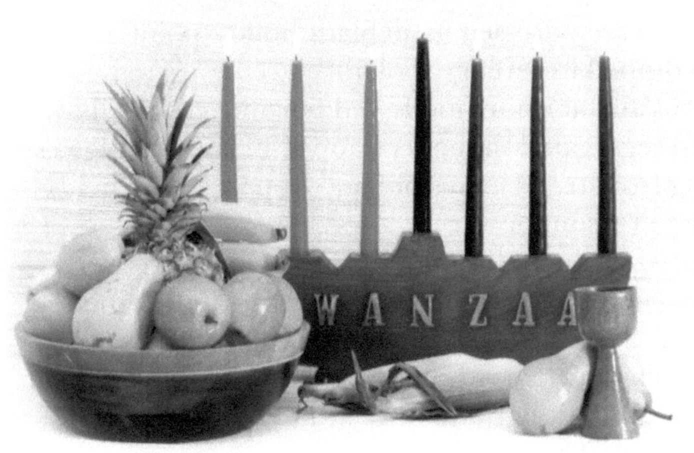
WANZAA

The Movement (poetry)

A slow creep dressed in all black hollow point
tips dipped in revenge look threw red eye's red
beams aim at white hoods and burning crosses that
burn segregated thoughts trapped in jail bars nigga,s
hang from tree's leaves of hate drop in cotton fields
grow a reason for war.
Dashikis stained with blood drips below the poverty
line 1out of 5 genocide drinks for free in the ghetto
bullets fly in a cloud of smoke crack cracks pieces
of black skin spins into Katrina winds blow November
skies shine a light to the white house! (HISTORY)
(Obama!) The Movement!

Osiris Halisi

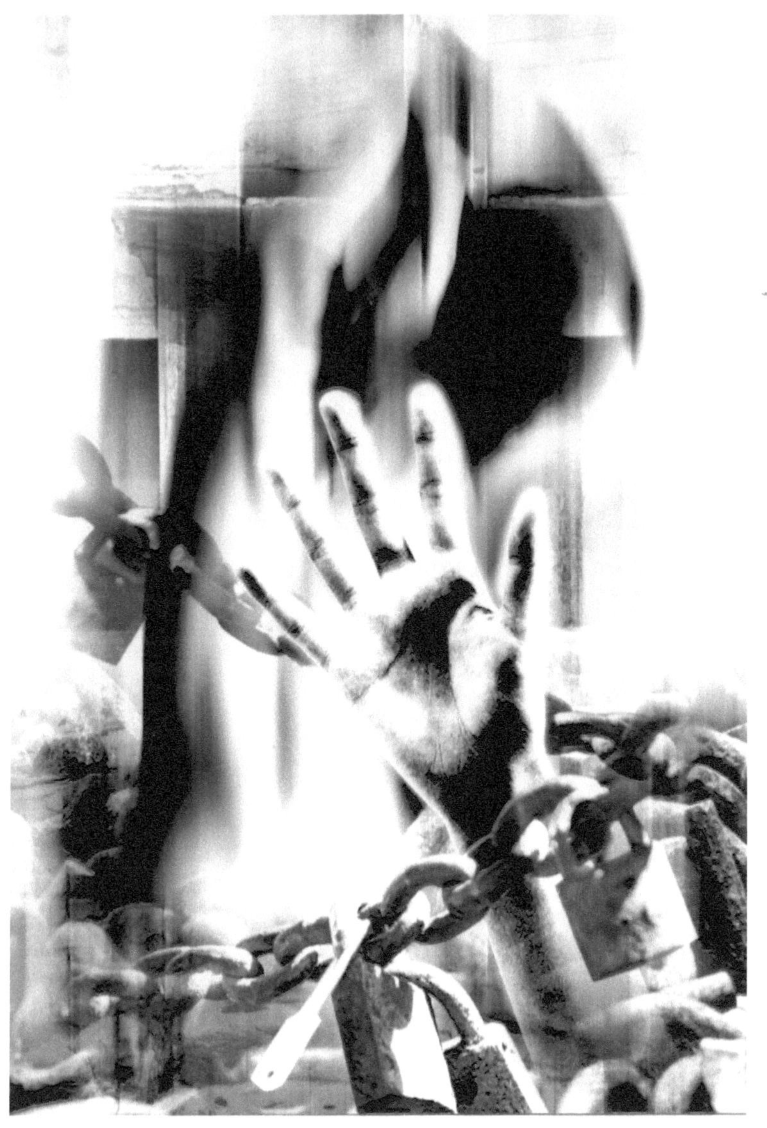

California

Being born in California is a blessing a gift from god seeing so many cultures, and different idea's about life you soak up so much game it helps. As a boy playing in the hills of Altadena exploring Pasadena streets, waiting for the moment I could walk on the pier at Santa Monica and run into the pacific ocean, and wash the rage of the city of angels away for the moment.

I wouldn't trade it for the world I have had the fortune to travel to many places with my father in his quest for knowledge, but out of all the places California is the best.

Writing in California sunshine so much of my poetry comes from Just that , drive slow! West coast Love!

Osiris Halisi

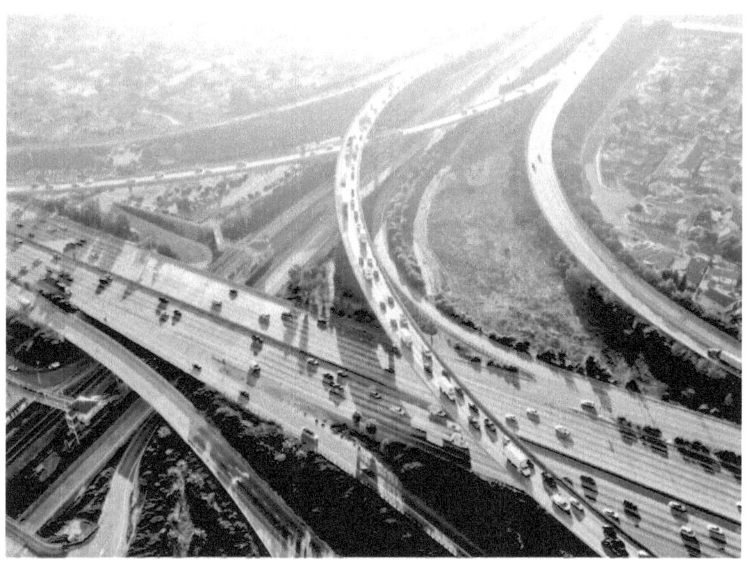

To live and die in California (poetry)

I have no choice my soul was baptized in the
sea born in the hills of Altadena my heart beats at
a pace were I can breathe the fresh air of Pasadena
skies, bullets fly aimed at red or blue and damn sure
Green.

Demands the sacrifice of fresh blood in the chase
for materials dreams were stars awake lost in the city
of angels and cameras flash forever young inhale the
smog of refusing to leave the gateway to heaven!

As hell is around the corner hiding behind palm tree's
blowing down Pasadena streets I blow tree's into a ocean
breeze my dreams play on California streets the last
place my mother smiled.

Osiris Halisi

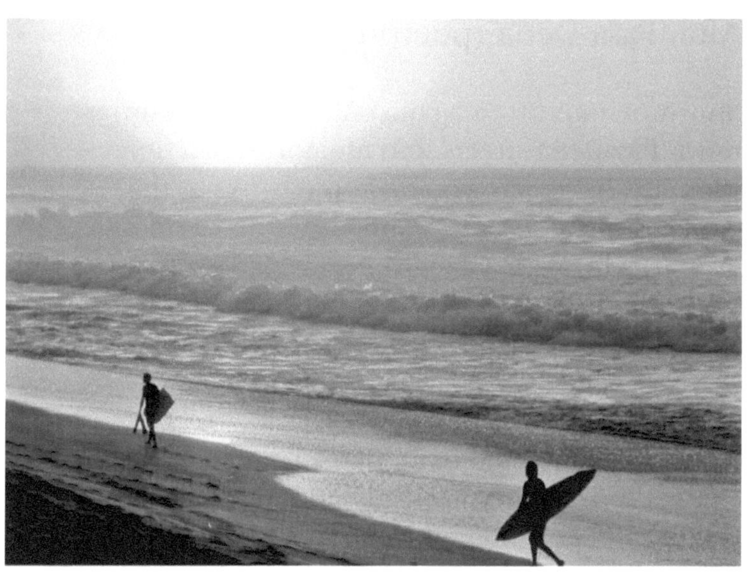

Alta/Pasa Dena (poetry)

Sunshine rain drops against Altadena hills run
down Pasadena streets into memories of a time
when my heart was whole, on the banks of the
Santa Monica pier my grand father tied a line
around a hook that caught my imagination and
my mothers laugh seemed to last forever and
a day.

My father pray for the knowledge of
a king lost in a book that open a page to a map
to the mother land, while me and my cousins
sat on solid ground and listen to a plan of a
organizations plan for a day that would come
in the winds of November skies 2008.Obama!

Candles burn on mantels and dashikis
stained with blood of the tears of women that gave
life to a struggle fought by men on California streets
were names changed but remained the same.

Lost on the borders of the city of angels my visions of
happiness echo's down Pasadena streets like a fast ball
thrown by a child or a touch down scored in a park
called Victory!
that must be a figment of my imagination I sit alone
looking for my angel lost in the city of angels I write
to my mothers voice! Lagary Newton 1947-2004 RIP

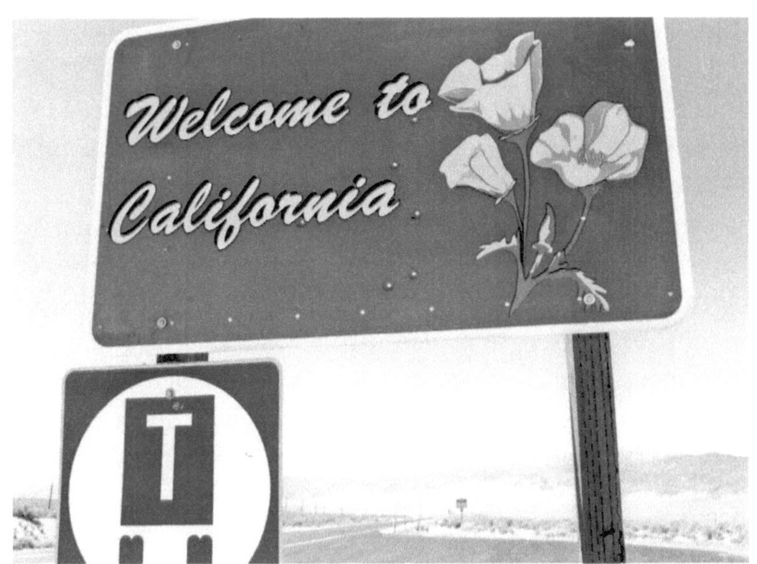
Welcome to
California
T

The cycle

Out of struggle are the scars that we pass to are children that often create a cycle of violence that can only becured by love!

You know I come from struggle and was born to hope held by the arms of those on the front lines of change when a black person did not have a chance so my father's struggle is also mines how to change anger into love, how to evolve, you can't intro duce your children to hell and assume that heaven will be in there's eye's at the end of violence is violence. Break the cycle!

Osiris Halisi

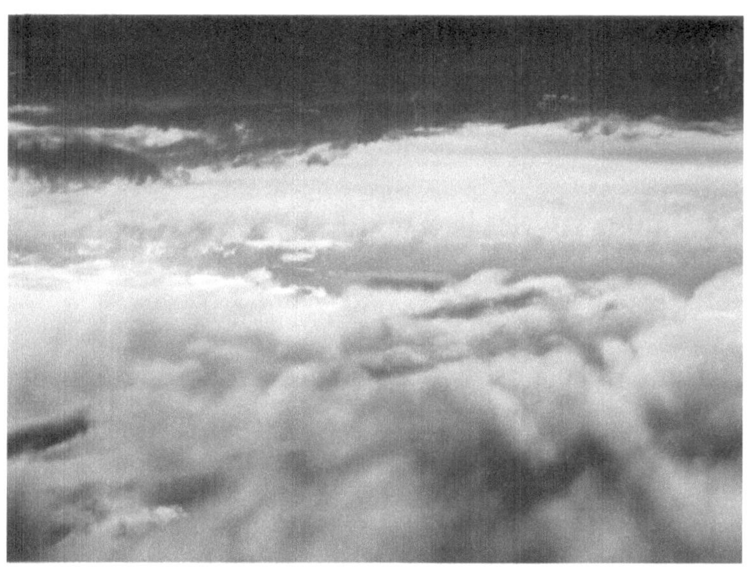

Small eye's (poetry)

Small eye's engaged on chaos as the screams of violence plays in or children's nightmares and every fist crashes threw the soul slowly starting a cycle that leads to a road that ends were you began lost in hells arms fighting to break free from what the eye's witness, anger begins to infect the heart fueled by hate, a child cries.

Small eye's engaged on chaos the murder of self esteem a mothers tear drop drips on the floor a little boy plays in the middle of war scars ever body that takes part.

Small eye's engaged on chaos ! We can not show are children hell and assume heaven will be in there eye's! don't try to find a excuse, we all make mistakes ! Love cures struggle!

Osiris Halisi

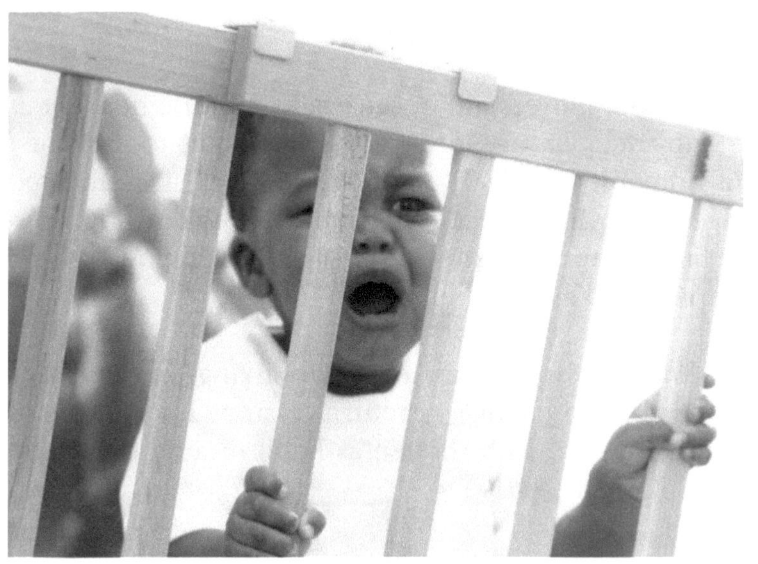

Waiting for the daylight

Gods children laid in the grass at midnight silent as a baby deer trying not to lose there souls to the worst of humanity, as black skin turns to black skies and red rivers run threw small children's minds and life slowly fades from the eye's of the next generation with no hope but to exist in hell

Waiting for the day to come walking on dirt roads starving for a chance to return to straw huts and mud floors infested with disease as babies watch there parents slowly die (HIV)

So little boys load full clips shooting at his brother because he couldn't hide from the hell of humanity genocide claims the life of the reflection in the mirror my ancestors home slowly fades.

I prayer to the children of Darfur !

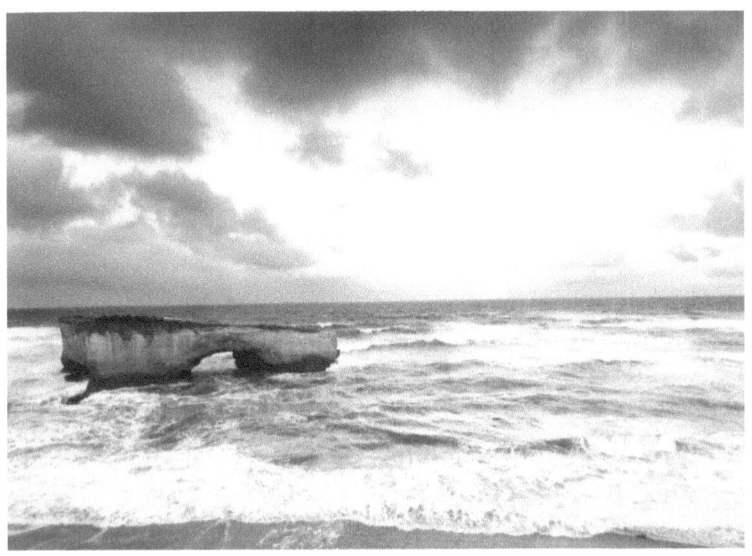

Indiana 1985

Bloomington Indiana the land of the Hoosiers! Corn fields and basketball courts covered with snow thirty minutes from the home of the Klu Klux Klan (Martinsville)

Just imagine coming from sunny California to the corn fields of Indiana, were nigga means nigger and the only black faces you see are at home. My first taste of the Midwest would stay with me forever , the first place I would understand what it meant to be black. My father was finishing his P.H.D and we moved to Bloomington Indiana in 1985 so he became a associate professor at IU and my world would change on the highways of 37, stuck on Lake Monroe my views would form as the day's slowly passed.

It was a love and hate relationship, I meet the best friends I ever knew and had the worst experiences in my life. I was a star player at Bloomington south my boys the b-town click Michael Blount, Murray Ross, Geno Devane, he always said he was going to be a doctor !(congratulations)

St. Mary's got a star! P. Knight I see you out there Texas Tech! Derrick Cross The coolest Mf in the world! Anthony Patton on TV I want to come back to New Orleans to.

The whole English family, Chris Collins , Marcus Courts, Skip and Doris and Tyrone. WoW

I think of Indiana all the Time on the banks of Santa Monica beach I sit and write poetry to a time long past, but never forgotten.

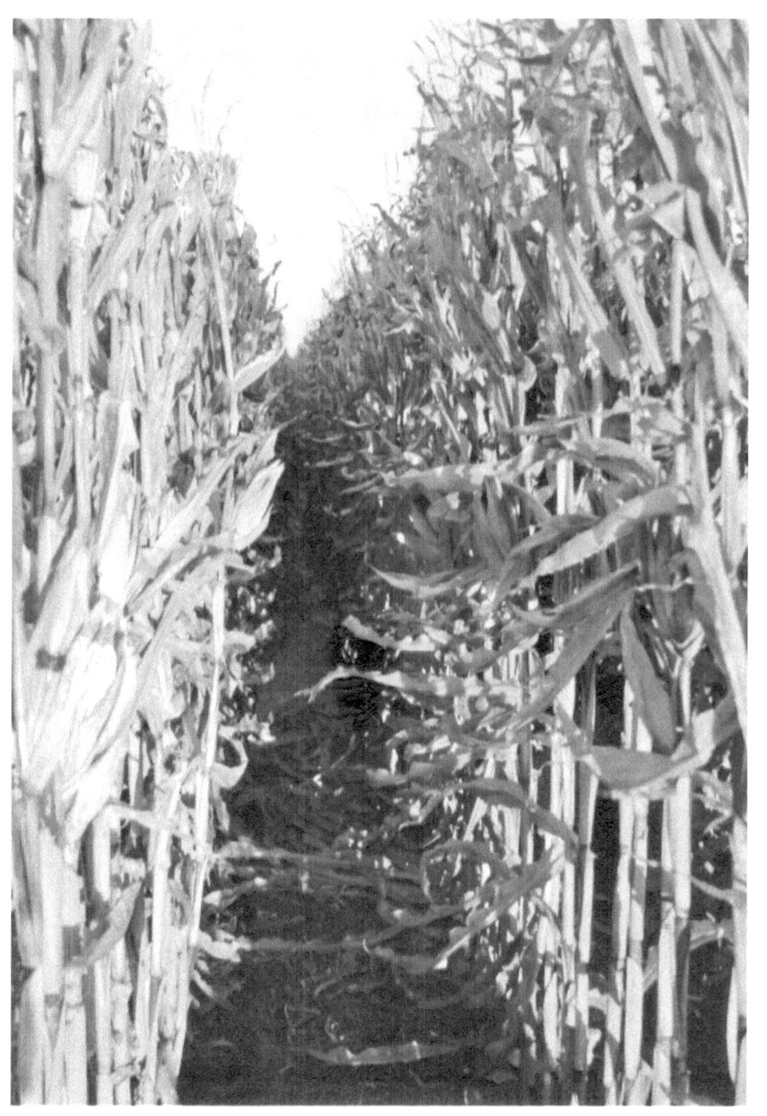

Bloomington

Heaven in the fall in the middle of assembly hall. The day's of Bobby knight a sea of red and white. A Keith Smart jump shoot finished by a Alfred lay up are may I say Scott May when IU ruled. The courts memories in the past fresh in my heart. Beats down Indiana streets I often think of you!
IU!

Osiris Halisi

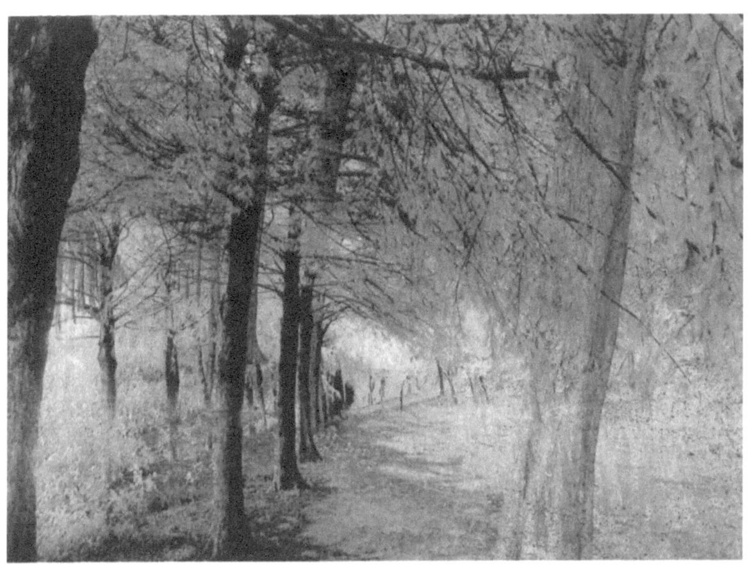

B- Town (poetry)

The land of the Hoosiers a basketball players dream
come true corn fields felled with the screams of my
ancestors screams covered by rebel flags and ford
trucks parked in trailer courts praying to leave the
trailer courts, little boys and girls shoot on courts
dressed in all red listening to a Bobby knight speech
A Melincamp song a brown county walk leaves fall
In the fall of the Midwest I reminisce at the sea shore
dressed in all red!

Osiris Halisi

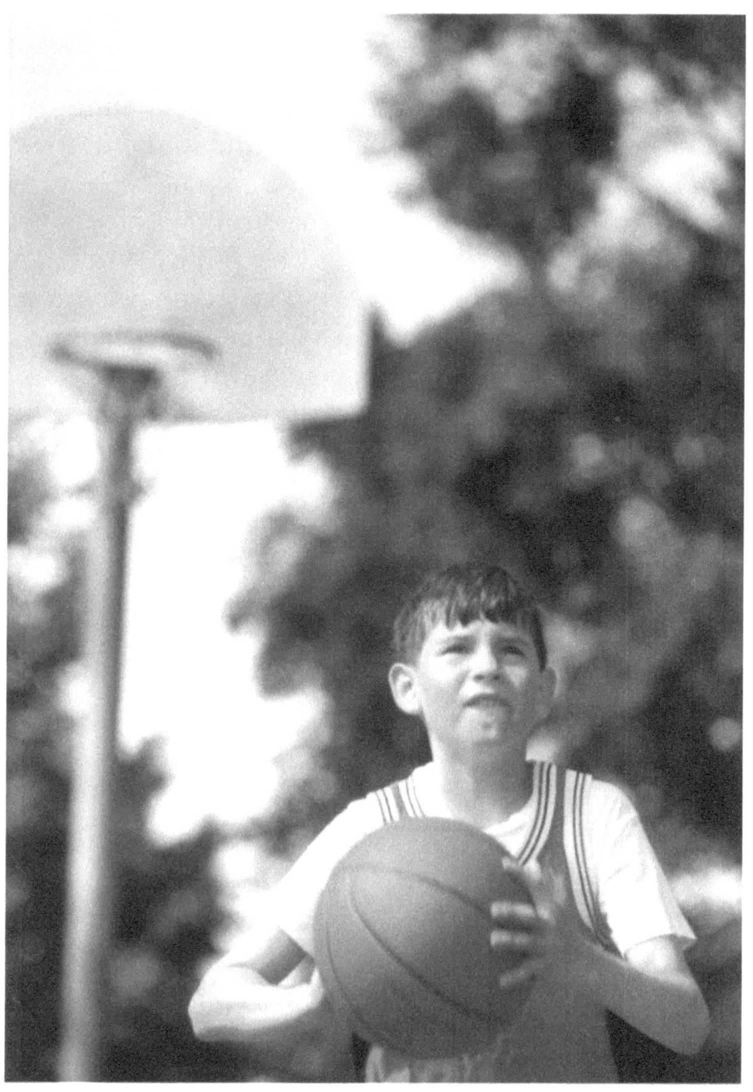

Army

The United States Army the place I lost my mind and fell in love with wearing Army green the sound of fresh cadence that keeps every soldier in step as each word prepared the mind for war . The Army has a strange way of making you forget about who you used to be. A drop out a problem child the son's Vietnam when you put on that uniform your part of something that feels real, especially if your not use to having a close family. I thought I had found my Purpose ! It was just the beginning of a journey that would take me from Ft. Sill OK to Garlstedt Germany and all over Europe memories that would make any young man smile believe me. I only had one problem! The Army is no place for free thinking, it's go hard or go home , no place for the depressed you must believe the body can lead the mind! It's not True?

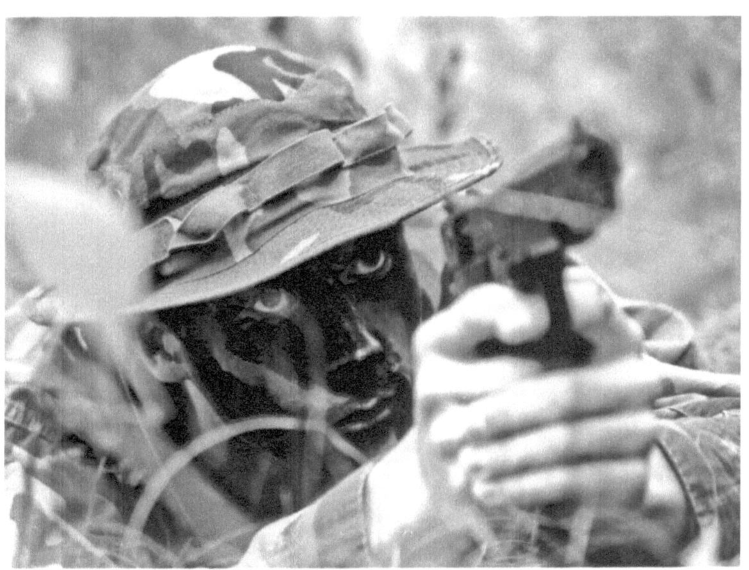

Suicide

The end of the line the death of hope
fades into night skies I begin to jump
what is life without love ? Goodbye,
all you need is God! Stay!

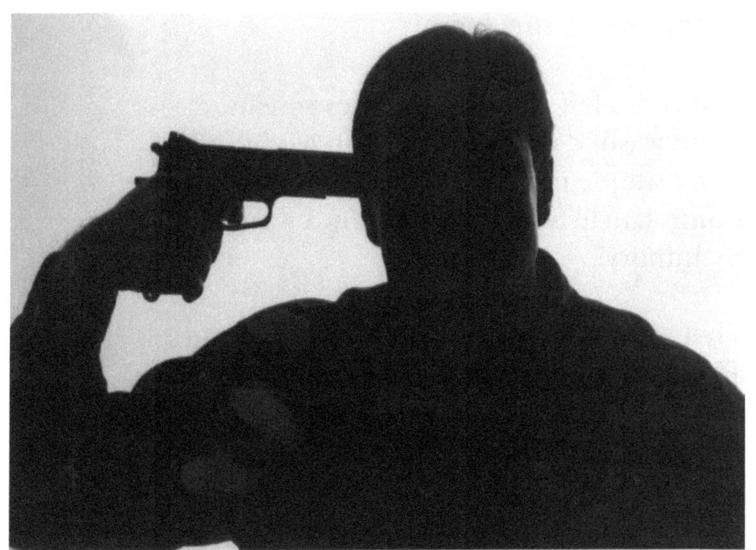

What about me (poetry)

Left right, left right is what they scream.
Brain washed that the body can lead the
Mind simple instructions just follow me!
Damn Uncle Sam I didn't know I would
Be hungry?

That war made me lose my mind , you put
That gun in my hand and I love my land but
I need a hand and then I will do it again United
We stand I hold signs saying feed me !

What about Me? Prayer to the veterans

Osiris Halisi

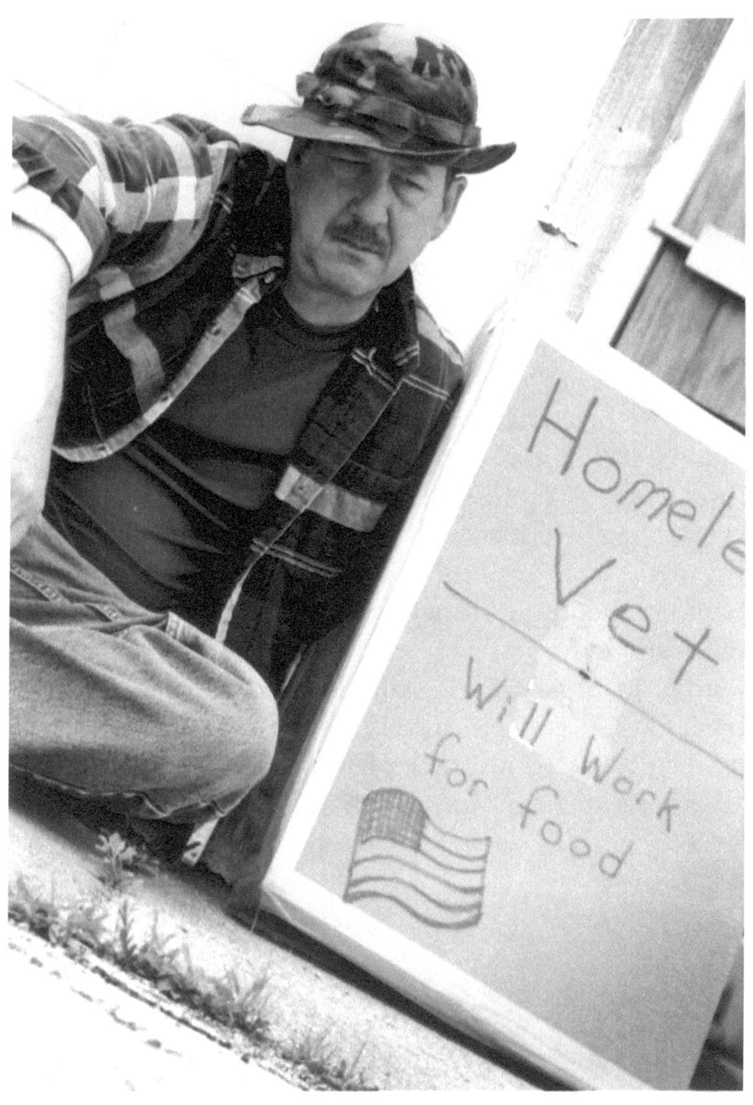

Atlanta

Atlanta Georgia the heart of the south a black mans paradise writing on the banks of Lake Lanier hustling on east point streets on the way to buck head collecting money on peach tree corners, chasing materials dreams falling in love with women sliding down poles. My addiction begins with gold teeth and dollar bills rolled to sniff lines in my road threw the evolution to black.

I had been going to Atlanta every since my cosine Masaba Tyson aka Capp one www.Addicted2clubs.com the owner of 2colds records and the only real pimp I every knew. He moved there when we were little boys I remember in his back yard we would catch lightning bugs crazy coming from California the dirty south summers are unforgettable! east point, the under ground, Piedmont Mount park , lake Lanier , six flags , crystal palace, follies, Houston's, buck head, masters, the old gold club, 112 , club anytime, woodland high, East point Chain gang, Bigg Gipp, trick, cool breeze, chief, wall street, tate, big slate, Rico, know my name. I love the ATL

Osiris Halisi

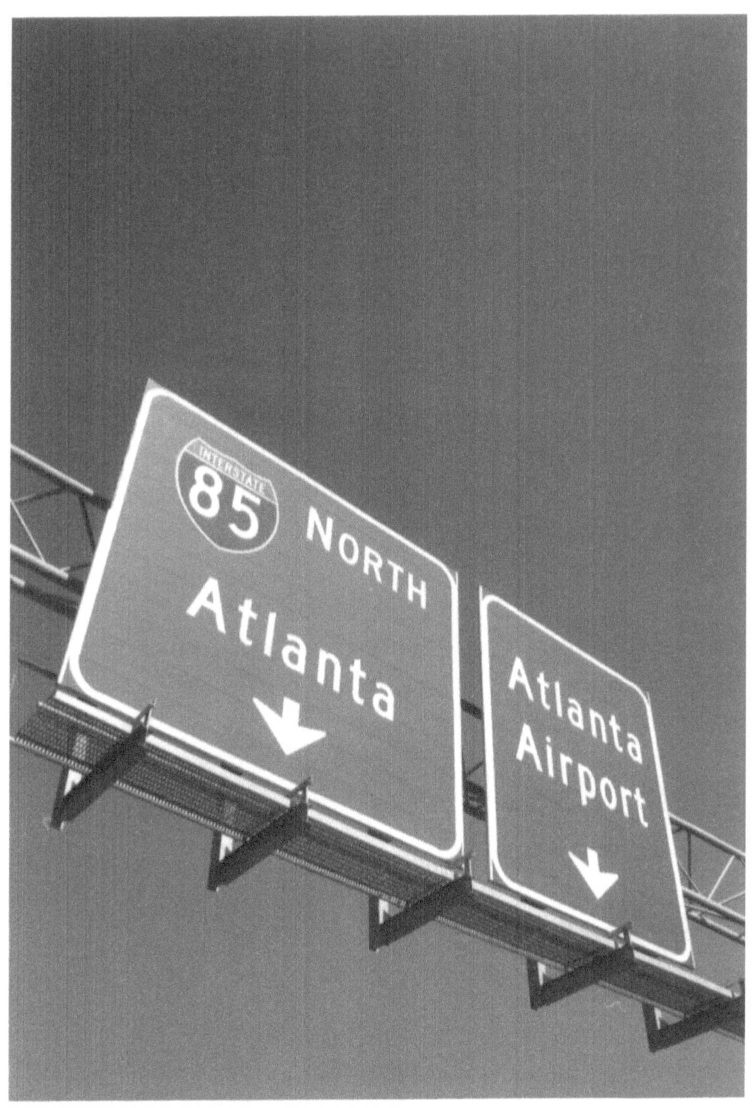

Street Music (poetry)

Fresh dressed pockets full rims spinning diamonds
mixed with gold linked to pyramids that say a king
must shine!

The perfect beat Hennessey and coke mixed
with the perfect smoke created by God so the
Sane do go insane.

Fully loaded not scared to squeeze laid back
In Cadillac system on blast to block the past
when niggas pick cotton to eat! trapped across
sea's sold for greed for the need of a race to
feel supreme.

I dress in all black and LA hat a blue flag and
Blow tree's in Altadena Hills you'll find me.
Street Music Osiris!

Osiris Halisi

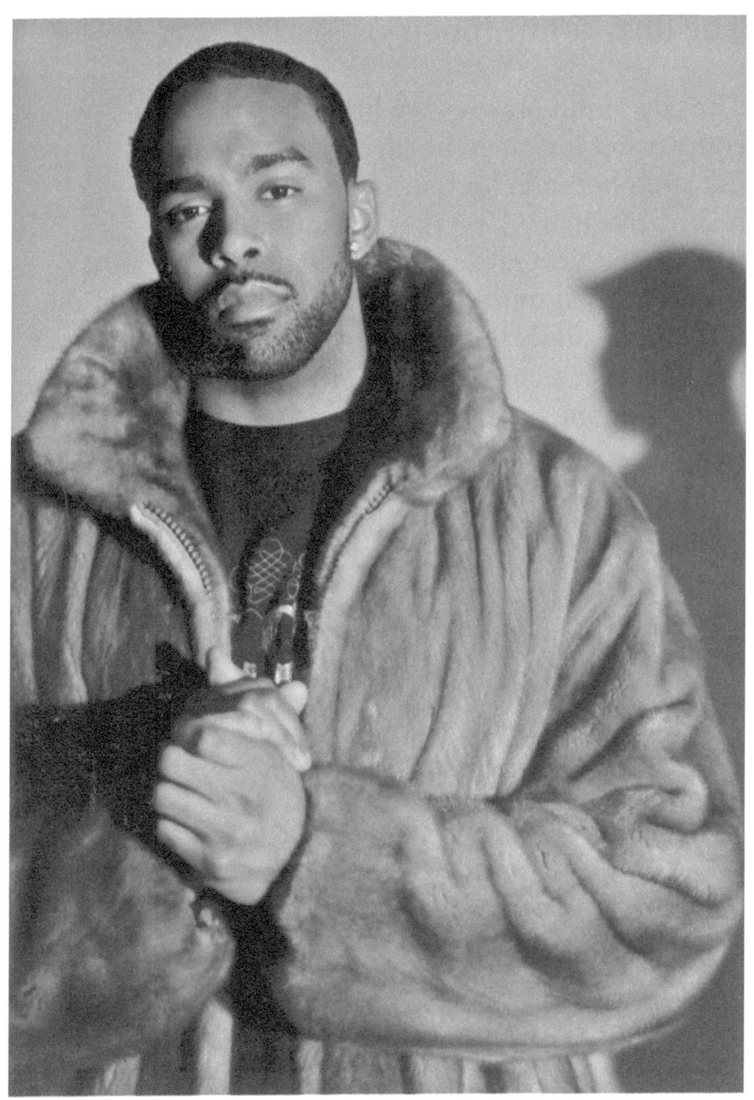

The dirty south (poetry)

The city of the braves were brave hearts live in country fields draped in rebel flags wave down I20 lanes between high ways threw the final resting place of a king that dreams will come true under November skies I ride down east point streets headed underground I found the heart of the dirty south slowly falling in love with magic cities ducking bullets at a club called gold I'm in love with a stripper calling me daddy and police sirens end at Clark county bars the city of angels is home I reminisce on red clay thinking of the dirty south.

Osiris Halisi

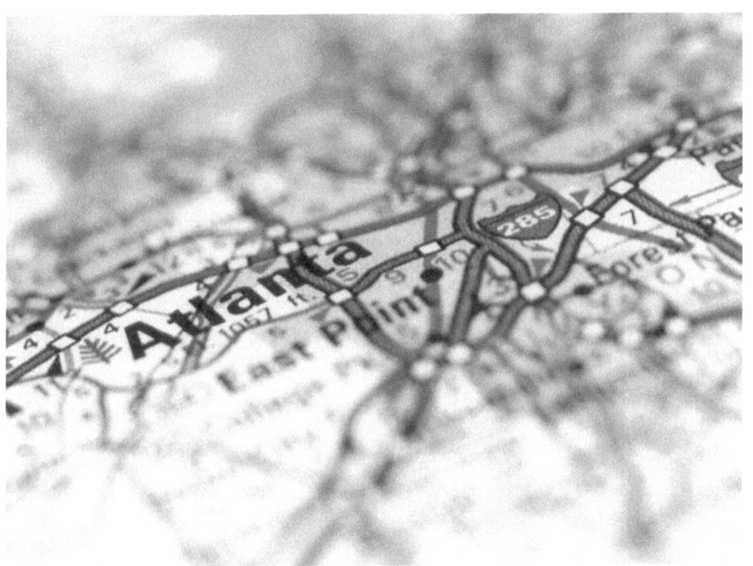

Trap Rules (poetry)

Everybody ain't your friend even if they got the same skin
my brother will put your ass to sleep so they can eat so
keep your heat in arms reach, and your bible in your hand
because a nigga will kill a black man in a blink of a eye
that's why some stay high when they ride down streets
were bullets fly and birds land broken into ounces sold
by the gram cracks in the wall inhaled in glass pipes steal
the souls of the under ground railroad slaves to a new Master. The Trap Atl!

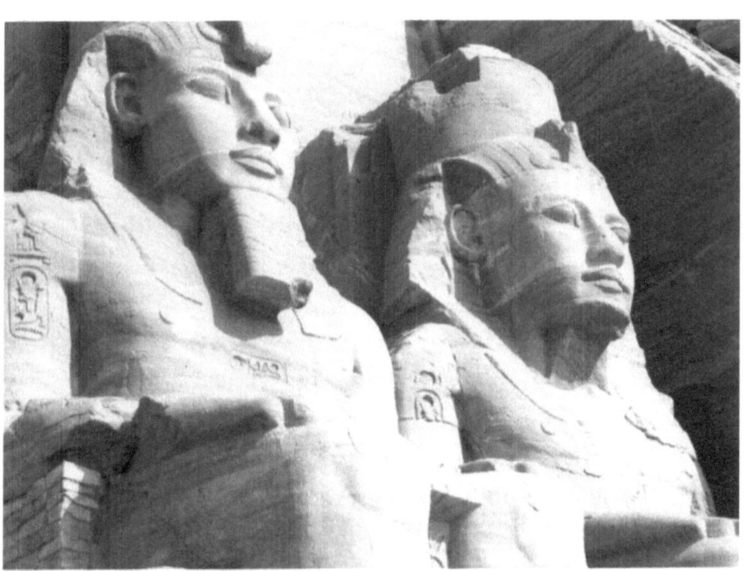

Letters to God

My whole life has been a letter to God, me writing on my knee's praying he hears me standing at the edge in love with the dark. Threw a cycle of violence my struggle with the depression and thoughts of suicide and the death of my mother was hard, I could Hear her whisper In my ear it's not how you start, it's how you finish.

Just believe and your dreams are possible, my search has always been for purpose what am I here for? My family all scholars and business men and women. Me a G.e.d a quarter key a scale and weekly hotel I sit alone writing poetry, what happen? When my mother died she was also battling with depression and hope.

Wondering what happened? I remember she always carried her bible and would tell me about God smiling? damn near homeless I would tell her I don't think God can hear you, she would laugh and smile and call me one Of my child hood names and say believe . I watched so Many people look at her with hate yet she still smiled I Couldn't Understand it . When she died I understood all you have is time, so love while you can. So I picked up her bible another scripture down on the way home I write letters to God.

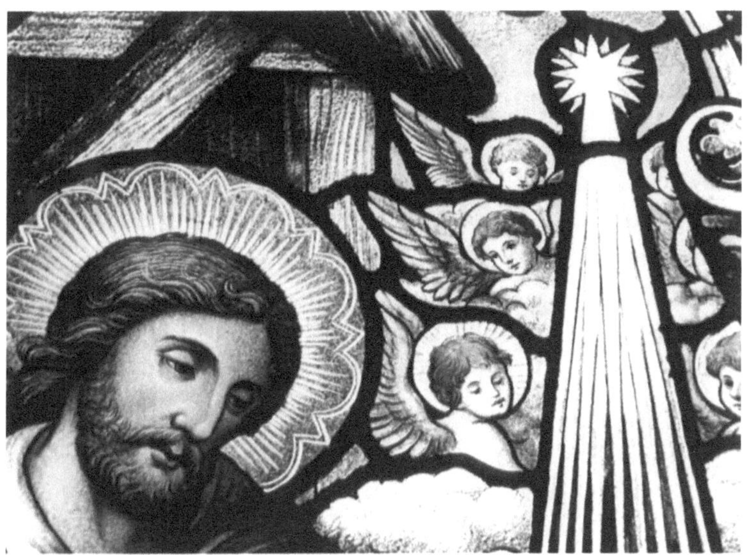

You still here? (poetry)

You are unconditional as my knee's drip blood
of the sins that dance in my nightmares wondering
why you love me?
I sit here with a blunt and full glass pouring my pain
away lost in cloud of smoke .
Your words sit on mantels and my mothers urn sit behind
candles that burn remembering her voice saying believe.
My heart beat slows to a pace were I can touch
the beauty of life and hear the sound of love I
Know your still here.

Grave yard tears (poetry)

Were is home graveyard tears grass grows clouds
Of pain when you breathe fresh air breezes blow
Your memory a dream in my sleep nightmares
Laugh laughter remembering you laugh I laugh
In my mind you live I die at your death I'm
Reborn in a childs eye your grandaughter looks
Like you. (LAGARY WAS HERE)

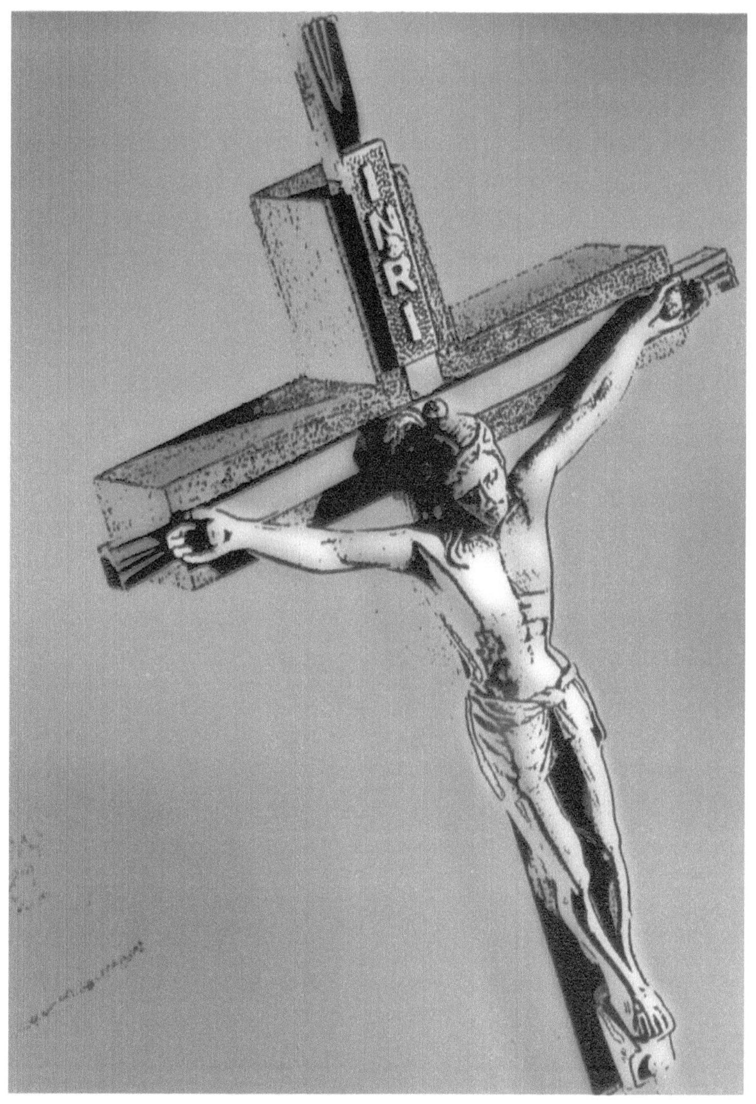
INRI

Never can say goodbye to my friends

What is death? But a memory that love does exist If only a moment in time my eye's could recognize your face which is now a picture in a frame and your ashes are the first thing I see when I open my eye's to a world that love one day will die . I can't wait to see you again in the wind I say your name
(LAGARY)

Osiris Halisi

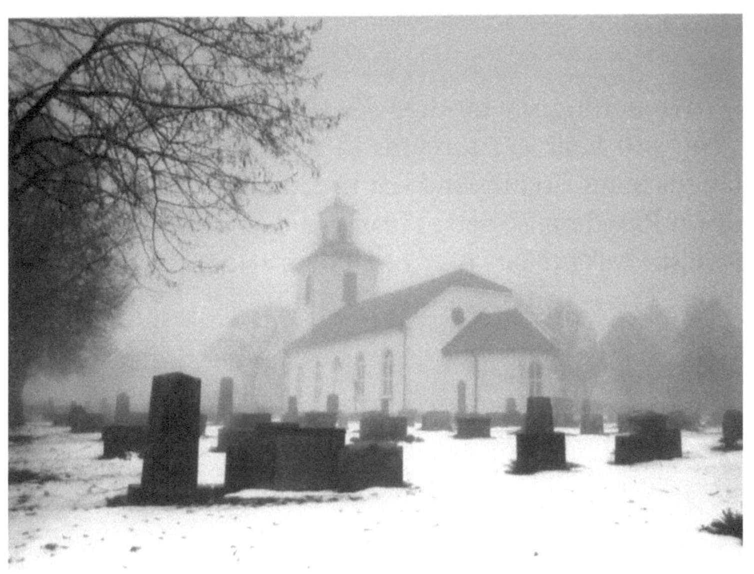

Cancer

Whatching my mother die from cancer was painful I can still hear her screams in my nightmares and her laughs in my dreams and her touch when the wind blows down Pasadena streets. Threw the lost of unconditional love she left me her pen and a blank page. I write to her voice. I miss you mom

Osiris Halisi

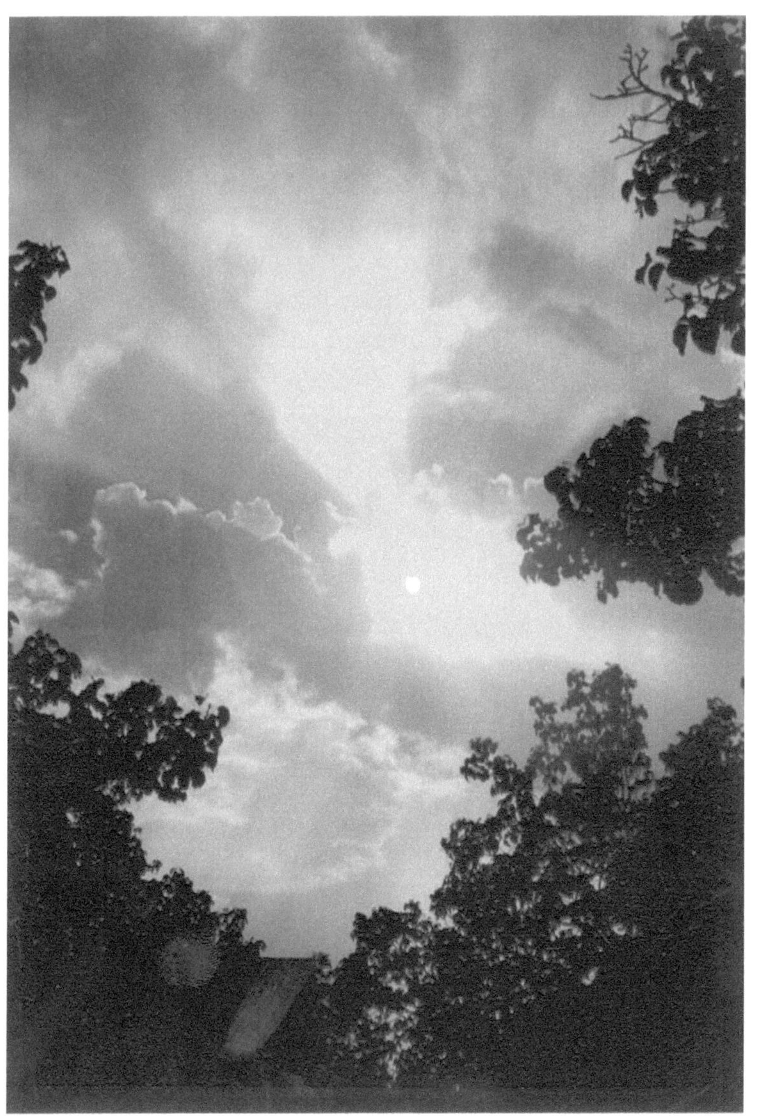

Keep holding on

A thief that can't be seen but slowly steals
the life out of a life that only last so long
preying on pain caused by life that we all
must live so don't waste it on fear.
I know that stare like your not there look
in the sky, tomorrow the sun will rise. Keep
Holding On. For the depressed a prayer!

Osiris Halisi

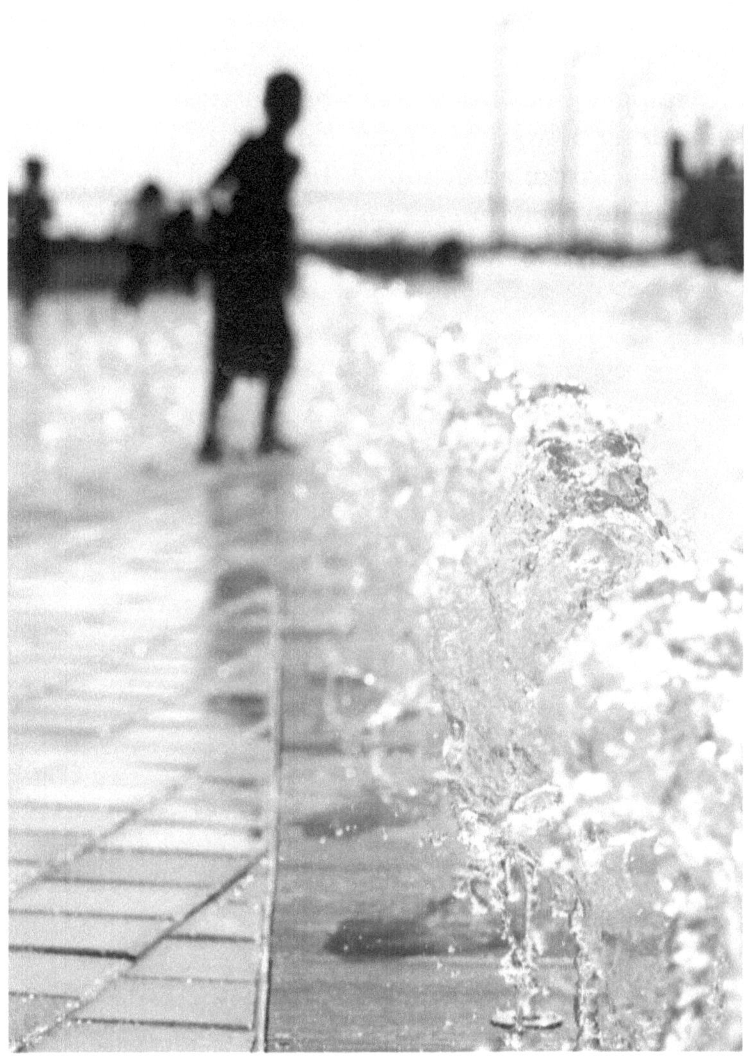

Addicted

Addicted to me means many things and when you
Are trapped in a enviroment when survival is the
Only thing on your mind the search to feel sane
Sometimes form addictions. I think we all are
Addicted to something as long as God is your
Final destination. (Survive)

Osiris Halisi

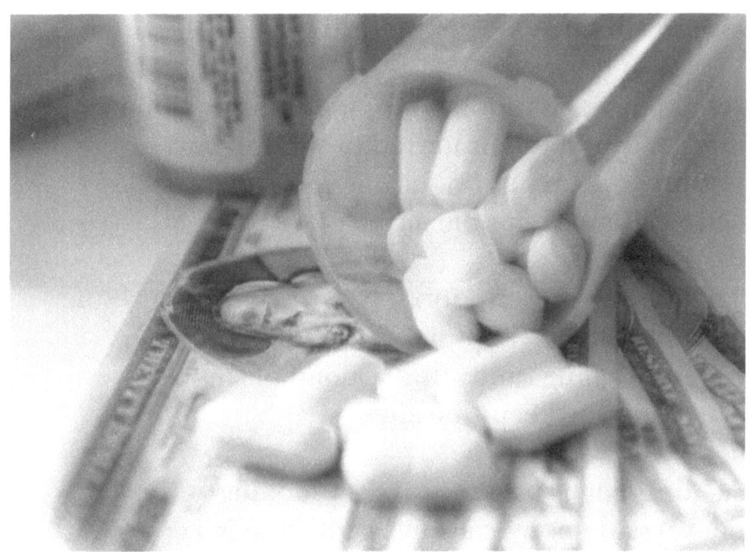

What kills me keeps me alive

Liquid in a glass addictions passed threw blood
lines as deadly as a hundred proof, the start
button to poetry as I pour one more glass.
what kills me keeps me alive!

That ghetto prescription sticky green a empty blunt
crumbled fire wet lips lick packed pain relievers
rolled exhaling sanity into a cloud of smoke.
What kills me keeps me alive!

At the edge of water falls, looking over cliffs of darkness demons call my name angels keep me from falling. What kills me keeps me alive.

Osiris Halisi

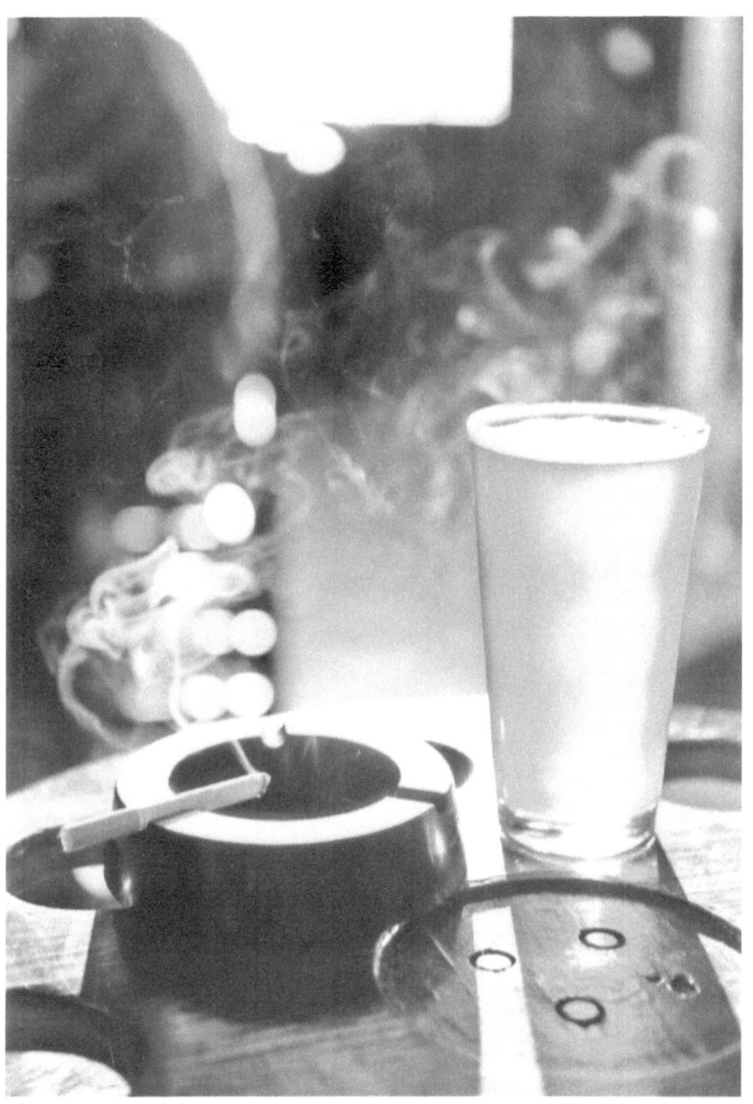

A wife, A mother, Your little girl

When a man loves a wife a mother or a child
It is complete of every part of every piece of
the heart that beats from the breath of a women
that exhales nine months long creating life a wife,
A mother or child the sound of a women's voice that
truly loves you can be recognized threw hell and hell
a man will travel to hear a wife a mother or
child that speaks his name.

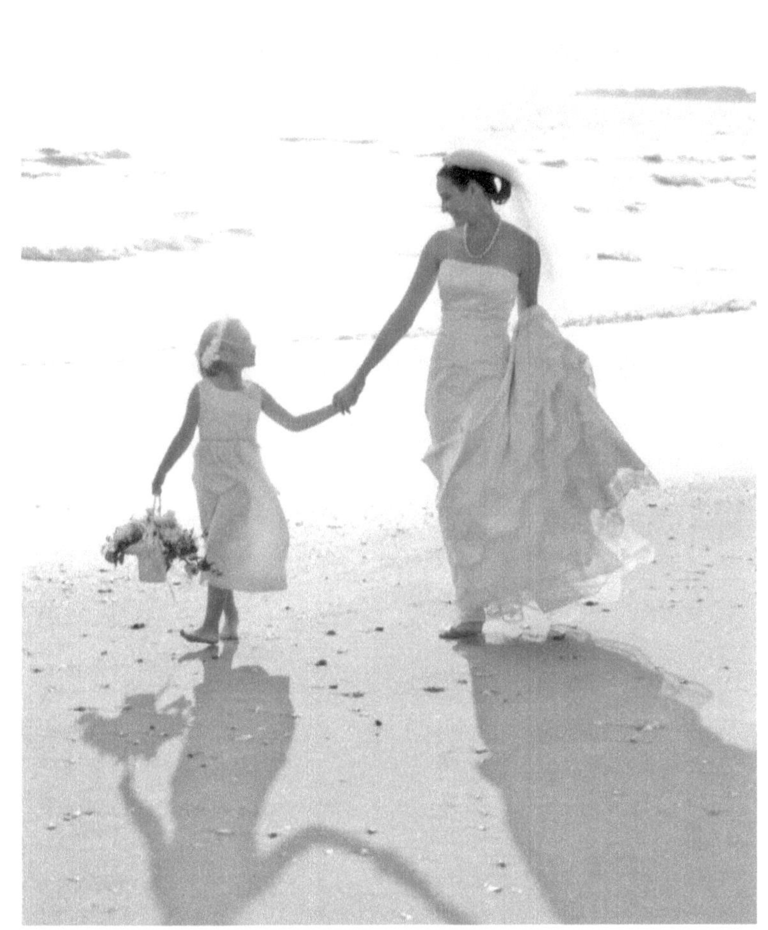

Hope (poetry)

A prayer in the mind the light of the soul the
Scars of change the tears of humanity the
Screams of struggle the blood of war the
Birth of a child the kiss of God the sunrise on
A new day. Hope!

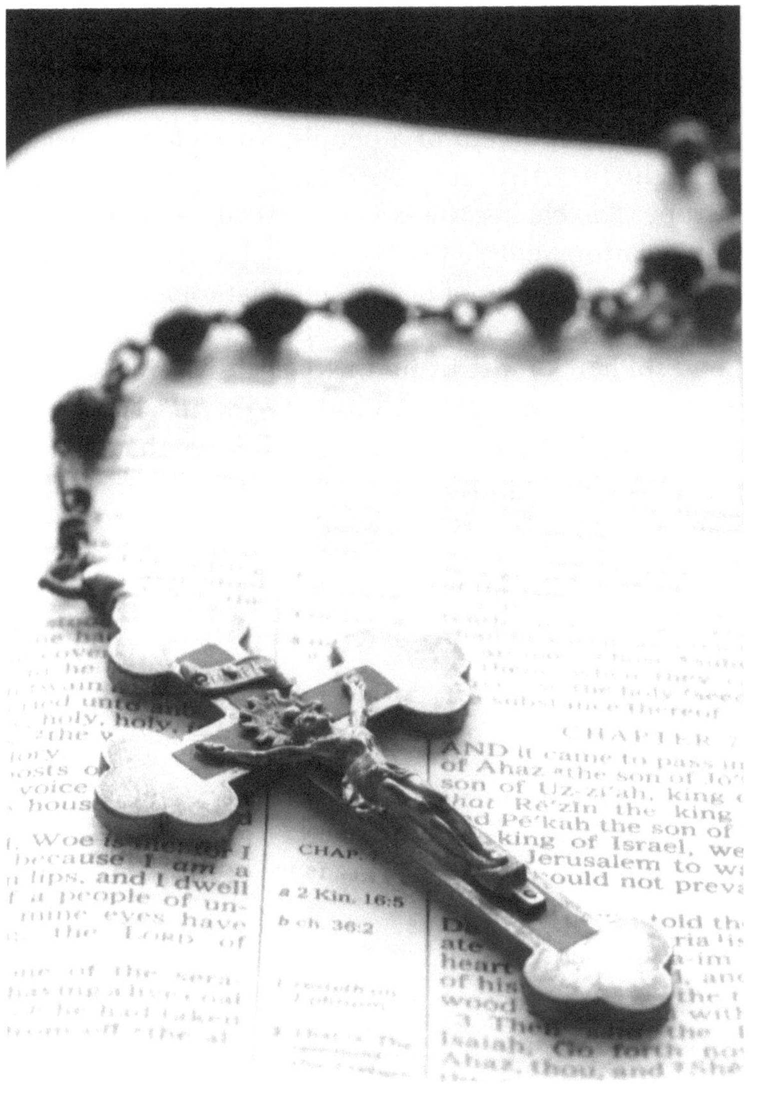
holy, holy,
Woe
and I dwell
people of un-
CHAP.
a 2 Kin. 16:5
b ch. 36:2
CHAPTER
AND it came to pass in
of Ahaz
son of Uz-zi'ah, king
Re'zin the king
Pe'kah the son of
king of Israel, we
Jerusalem to w
ould not prev
Isaiah, Go forth

November Skies

November skies is a dedication to Barrack Obama for fulfilling a dream of a peoples struggle that began when the first African stepped on American soil bound by ropes and chains, this is a prayer to all those lost souls lost in cotton fields, a tear for my ancestors. A prophecy come to light spoke of by the king that told a tell of the promise land. To my father Halisi and my mother Mutamu soldiers on the front line of the Civil rights movement. The hope that the winds of Katrina Will never blow again. To all those little black faces that Benefit from the blood of those that came before them. To The new black king Barrack Obama .

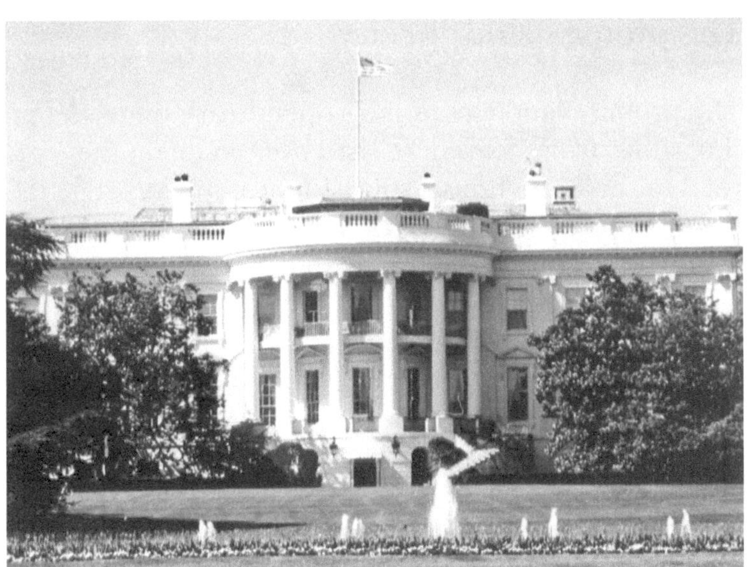

The promise land (poetry)

The promise land closed eye's open hearts angels
sing songs from heaven we shall over come on the
road to the white house, spirits sit in tree's looking
threw Gods eye's the sun rises to a new day black skin
white clouds brown sand a peoples blood a movement
of love.
A color blind sky repairs Katrina winds the revolution
Begins on the road threw cotton fields my ancestors
Speak in November skies the new Black king is
crowned.
OBAMA2008!

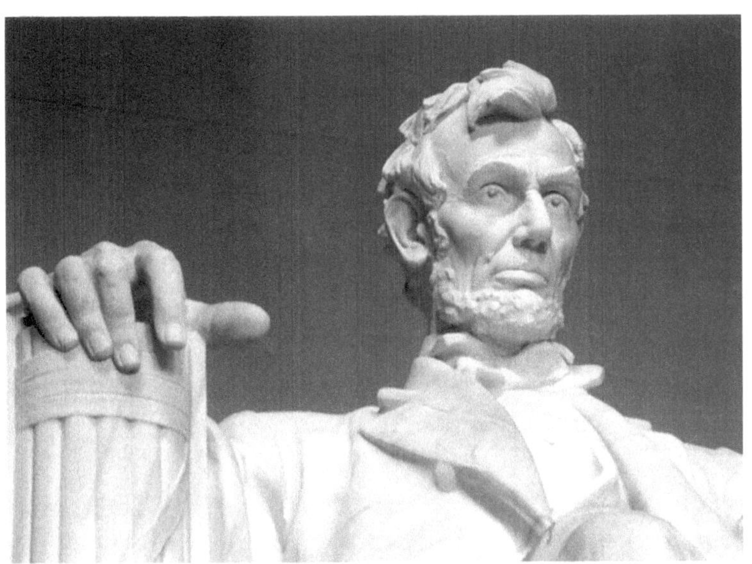

Evolve (poetry)

I sit alone under blue skies and watch my children
play blood stain memories dance in my mind suicide
thoughts disappear at my mothers grave angels whisper
In my ear love songs I sing never give up on your
dreams I dream of a new day with a blank page I
pray for tears caused by me vanish with my pain I
bleed I'm sorry all I can say, a few stand by my side
I write under tree's while Pasadena wind Blows I
Blow tree's to life. To the hopeless keep going!

Osiris Halisi

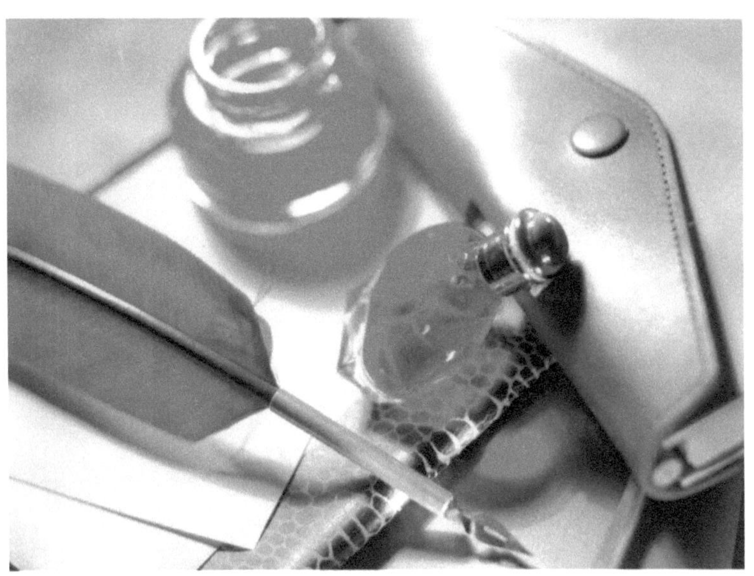

www.ingramcontent.com/pod-product-compliance
Lightning Source LLC
Chambersburg PA
CBHW021902170526
45157CB00005B/1929

* 9 7 8 1 4 3 9 2 3 5 2 0 1 *